Wizards

by Grace Hansen

abdobooks.com

Published by Abdo Kids, a division of ABDO, P.O. Box 398166, Minneapolis, Minnesota 55439.
Copyright © 2023 by Abdo Consulting Group, Inc. International copyrights reserved in all countries.
No part of this book may be reproduced in any form without written permission from the publisher.
Abdo Kids Jumbo™ is a trademark and logo of Abdo Kids.

Printed in China

052022

092022

 THIS BOOK CONTAINS RECYCLED MATERIALS

Photo Credits: Alamy, Everette Collection, Getty Images, Shutterstock,
©PicturePrince p.7/ CC BY-SA 4.0

Production Contributors: Teddy Borth, Jennie Forsberg, Grace Hansen
Design Contributors: Candice Keimig, Pakou Moua

Library of Congress Control Number: 2021950564
Publisher's Cataloging-in-Publication Data

Names: Hansen, Grace, author.

Title: Wizards / by Grace Hansen.

Description: Minneapolis, Minnesota : Abdo Kids, 2023 | Series: World of mythical beings | Includes online
    resources and index.

Identifiers: ISBN 9781098261931 (lib. bdg.) | ISBN 9781098262778 (ebook) | ISBN 9781098263195
    (Read-to-Me ebook)

Subjects: LCSH: Wizards--Juvenile literature. | Witches--Juvenile literature. | Magic--Juvenile literature. |
    Folklore--Juvenile literature. | Legends--Juvenile literature.

Classification: DDC 133.4--dc23

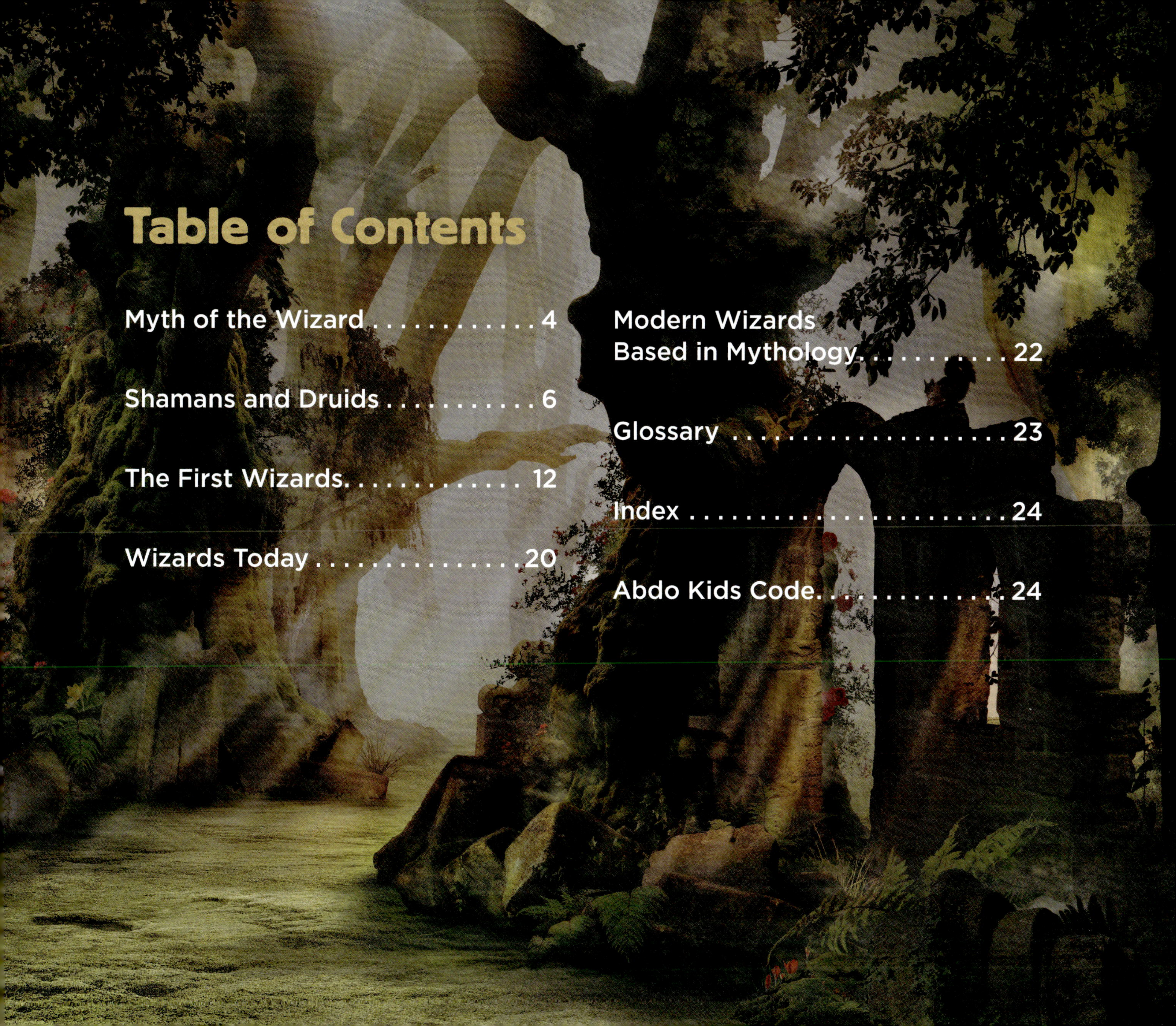

Table of Contents

Myth of the Wizard

A wizard is a legendary, powerful being who practices magic. Wizards are often kind and good, but can also be evil.

Shamans and Druids

The idea of wizards may go back 15,000 years to when **shamans** first practiced. More recently, **Celtic** druids were the closest people to wizards in society.

7

Druids paid attention to the cycles in nature. They knew the best times to plant crops and when to go to war. Druids also claimed to be able to see the future.

9

When the Romans took over Britain in 43 CE, druids still practiced quietly. They passed down what they knew from **generation** to generation. In 400 CE, the Roman empire fell. Around this time the legend of King Arthur rose.

The First Wizards

In some stories, King Arthur had a special, magical adviser named Merlin. Merlin was likely based on the druids. He is one of the first known **fictional** wizards.

13

Like Merlin, wizards are often shown as wise, older men who give good advice. In fact, the word *wizard* comes from the Middle English word *wys* meaning "wise."

Wizards often have white hair, long beards, and are dressed in cloaks. But most notably, wizards have magical abilities. They are usually born able to do magic. They study and practice constantly to perfect it.

Though wizards are very powerful, they also have limits. They cannot easily fix every problem. Many of their **spells** are dangerous if done incorrectly.

Wizards Today

After Merlin, many other beloved wizards came into the world. From Gandalf of *Lord of the Rings* to Harry Potter, wizards continue to capture our imaginations.

Modern Wizards Based in Mythology

Jafar
Disney's *Aladdin*

- Evil sorcerer
- Knows how to make potions and can see the future
- Granted a wish by a genie to become more powerful

Kamek
Mario franchise

- A wizard who cares for the evil Bowser
- Knows many magical spells
- Can duplicate himself, fly, and teleport

Stephen Strange
Marvel character

- A talented medical doctor and master of magic
- Studied with the Ancient One to learn sorcery
- Can perform many spells, including creating portals

Glossary

Celtic – relating to the Celts who were members of any of the Indo-European peoples whose language is Celtic, such as the Irish, Scottish, Welsh, or Bretons.

fictional – existing only in a made-up story.

generation – an entire group of people who were born at the same time.

portal – a magical passageway to another place or time.

shaman – a priest or healer believed to have contact with the supernatural.

sorcerer – one who is believed to have supernatural powers aided by evil spirits.

spell – a word or group of words used to work magic.

wise – having understanding and good judgment about what is true or good.

Index

Abdo Kids
ONLINE
FREE! ONLINE MULTIMEDIA RESOURCES

Visit **abdokids.com** to access crafts, games, videos, and more!

Use Abdo Kids code **WWK1931** or scan this QR code!